D1209350

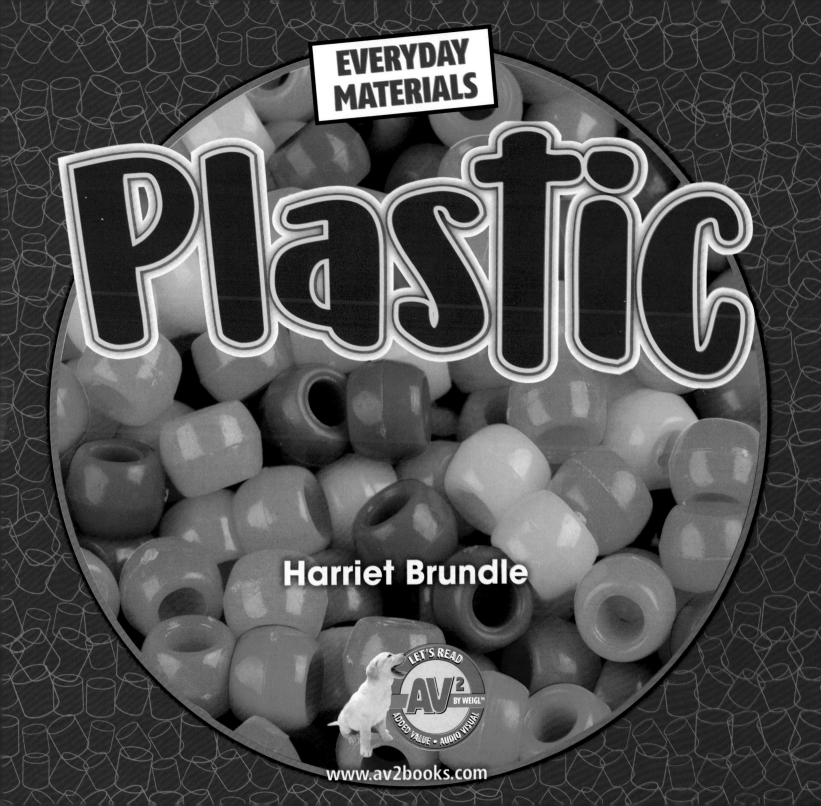

EVERYDAY MATERIALS

Plastic

Harriet Brundle

www.av2books.com

LET'S READ
AV²
BY WEIGL™
ADDED VALUE • AUDIO VISUAL

Go to **www.av2books.com**,
and enter this book's
unique code.

BOOK CODE

L B R 2 7 9 2 4

AV² by Weigl brings you media
enhanced books that support
active learning.

AV² provides enriched content that supplements and complements this book. Weigl's AV² books strive to create inspired learning and engage young minds in a total learning experience.

Your AV² Media Enhanced books come alive with...

Audio
Listen to sections of
the book read aloud.

Video
Watch informative
video clips.

Embedded Weblinks
Gain additional information
for research.

Try This!
Complete activities and
hands-on experiments.

Key Words
Study vocabulary, and
complete a matching
word activity.

Quizzes
Test your knowledge.

Slide Show
View images and
captions, and prepare
a presentation.

... and much, much more!

Published by AV² by Weigl
350 5th Avenue, 59th Floor New York, NY 10118
Website: www.av2books.com

Library of Congress Control Number: 2017960044

ISBN 978-1-4896-7392-3 (hardcover)
ISBN 978-1-4896-7843-0 (softcover)
ISBN 978-1-4896-7393-0 (multi-user eBook)

Printed in the United States of America in Brainerd, Minnesota
1 2 3 4 5 6 7 8 9 0 21 20 19 18 17

122017
120117

Project Coordinator: Jared Siemens Designer: Nick Newton

Weigl acknowledges Getty Images, Alamy, and Shutterstock as the primary image suppliers for this title.

Contents

AV² Book Code.................................... 2

What Is a Material?........................... 4

What Is Plastic?............................... 7

Properties of Plastic 8

Uses of Plastic 11

Plastic in Water............................... 12

Plastic in Heat 15

Plastic Toys 16

Musical Instruments...................... 19

Recycling Plastic............................ 20

Quiz 22

Key Words/log on to
www.av2books.com 24

3

What Is a Material?

Materials are what things are made of. Some materials are natural and some are man-made.

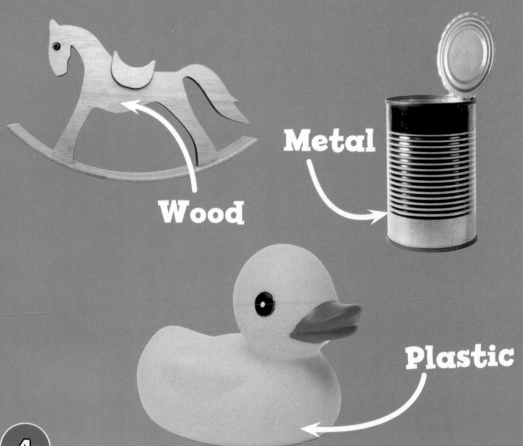

Wood

Metal

Plastic

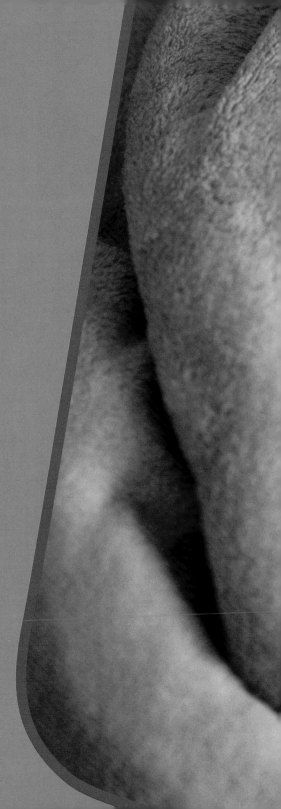

Every material has its own properties. A material might be very soft. This would be one of its properties.

TRY THIS!
What things in your home are soft?

What Is Plastic?

Plastic is a man-made material. Plastic is very useful because it can be used to make lots of different things.

When plastic is made, it is shaped into the object that is being made. Once the plastic is set, it can not be changed unless it is melted.

TRY THIS!
Have a look around the classroom. What can you see that is made from plastic?

Properties of Plastic

Some plastic is very strong and not bendy. Strong plastic is very useful for making lunch boxes.

Other types of plastics are light and bendy. The bags that we carry our shopping in are made of this type of plastic.

TRY THIS!
Can you think of types of plastics that are very hard? What kind of plastic is soft?

Uses of Plastic

Chairs and tables in the garden can be made from plastic. The plastic is strong but light so we can move it easily.

Bottles that we drink from are made of plastic. They are easily bent and squeezed.

Every minute **1 million plastic bottles** are purchased around the world.

Plastic in Water

Unlike some other materials, when plastic gets wet the water has no effect. It stays on the surface and can be easily wiped away. This is because plastic is waterproof. Raincoats are made of plastic to protect us from rainwater.

Plastic in Heat

When plastic is heated to a very high temperature, it will melt.

When the plastic has been melted, it can be turned into a different shape. Once it cools, the plastic is hard again!

🌎 Map Fact

Since 2016, North Carolina has seen a 2 percent increase in recycled bottles. They are expecting that number to grow.

Plastic Toys

Lots of different toys are made from plastic because it is light but strong.

Buckets and shovels are made of plastic. They are light so they can be carried, but are strong enough to lift the sand.

The most popular **plastic doll** is **Barbie**. More than **94 billion** Barbies are sold each year.

TRY THIS!
How many different toys can you think of that are plastic?

17

Musical Instruments

Some musical instruments are made of plastic. A recorder is a plastic tube with holes in it. When air is blown through the recorder, the instrument makes a noise. When the holes are covered, the instrument makes a different sound.

TRY THIS!
Plastic can also be found in the kitchen. How many kitchen items are plastic in your home?

Recycling Plastic

Some plastic can be recycled, which means we use it again. It is important that we recycle to help protect our planet.

When plastic is recycled, it can be made into new shapes. Plastic bottles can be turned into garden chairs!

Recycling just **one plastic bottle** saves the **energy** it takes to run a 100-watt light bulb for **four hours**.

Quiz

1.

Once a plastic is set, it can only be changed when what is done to it?

a) It is soaked in water
b) It is melted
c) It is frozen

3.

When plastic is recycled, what can be done to it?

a) Recycling makes it disappear
b) It can be turned into new shapes
c) It can be turned into paper

2.

What are raincoats made from?

a) Plastic
b) Cotton
c) Rubber

5.

Why are toys made from plastic?

a) Because plastic is light and strong

b) Because plastic is pretty

c) Because plastic smells good

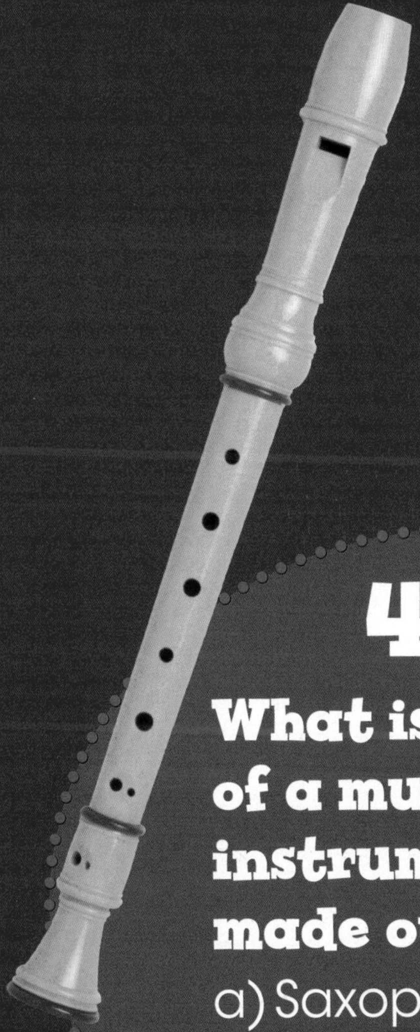

4.

What is an example of a musical instrument that is made out of plastic?

a) Saxophone

b) Recorder

c) Harp

KEY WORDS

Research has shown that as much as 65 percent of all written material published in English is made up of 300 words. These 300 words cannot be taught using pictures or learned by sounding them out. They must be recognized by sight. This book contains 98 common sight words to help young readers improve their reading fluency and comprehension. This book also teaches young readers several important content words, such as proper nouns. These words are paired with pictures to aid in learning and improve understanding.

Page	Sight Words First Appearance
4	a, and, are, is, made, man, of, some, things, what
5	be, every, has, home, in, its, might, one, own, this, very, would, your
7	around, because, being, can, different, from, have, into, it, look, make, once, see, set, that, the, to, when, you
8	carry, for, hard, kind, light, not, other, our, think, we
11	but, move, so, they, world
12	again, away, been, grow, high, no, number, on, turned, us, water, will
16	each, enough, more, most, than
17	how, many
19	air, also, found, sound, through, with
20	four, help, important, just, means, new, run, use, which
22	only, paper
23	an, example, good, out, why

Page	Content Words First Appearance
4	material, metal, plastic, wood
7	classroom
8	lunch boxes, shopping
11	bottles, chairs, garden, tables
12	raincoats, rainwater, surface, waterproof
15	North Carolina, recycled, temperature
16	Barbie, buckets, doll, sand, shovels, toys
19	holes, instruments, kitchen, noise, recorder, tube
20	bulb, energy, planet, recycled, shapes

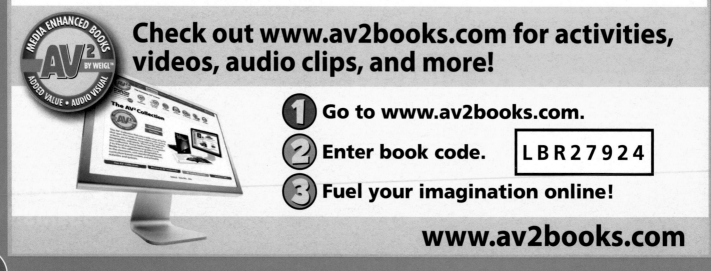